BUY SMART INSURANCE

Everything You Need To Know About Insurance

By Al Kash, LUTCF

ISBN: 978-1-941645-41-3

Designed and Published by:
Speakeasy Publications
73-03 Bell Blvd #10
Oakland Gardens, NY 11364

(888) 225-8594

DISCLAIMER

This publication is intended to be informational only. No legal advice is being given, and no agent-client relationship is intended to be created by reading this material.

Al Kash, LUTCF
17702 Mitchell North
Irvine, CA 92614
License #: 0E26238
(949) 216-3620

TABLE OF CONTENTS

AUTHOR INTRODUCTION

Al Kash got his first license in 2003 and has been in the insurance business for around 12 years. His office is in Irvine, California.

His agency began in 2005 as the Farmers insurance agency. When the agency started they began forming relationships with people, local business owners in particular, both locally and in South Orange County area.

Farmers Insurance Group was a multi-insurer company, so they tried to help families and business owners with all their needs in regards to insurance. This gained them access to other markets of insurance, after which they were contracted by multiple carriers.

The market has expanded a lot in the past 10 years, and they have access to multiple carriers. In many cases they are able to help people get the best insurance they need as far as what they want covered, and for the best prices available out in the market.

Al Kash's desire to help people got him into the insurance business. He likes being able to help people not lose their assets and to have a plan for their future and protect themselves and their family against unforeseen events.

Types Of Insurance Coverage Offered At Kash Insurance Agency

Personal-Line

Kash Insurance Agency is a one stop shop for their clients. They cover everything as far as insurance and they try to be a service oriented based company and agency.

Different departments at Kash Insurance Agency handle personal line insurances, including auto insurance, home owners insurance, umbrella insurance, investment properties, and life insurance. Those are on the personal line as well as some specialties such as motorcycle, boats and travel, etc.

Business-Line

The commercial department covers business insurances, which include general liabilities, business owner policies, commercial insurance, and workers' compensation. They also cover professional liabilities for doctors and lawyers.

Kash Insurance also has a department which covers employee benefits, including medical insurance or dental insurance, and other employee benefit plans that are provided by the employer.

Other Services Provided

Working with Kash Insurance not only gives people and business owners peace of mind, it also provides them with the tools that well help them both save money and make more money. This is why families, business owners, and professionals come to Kash Insurance.

What Makes Kash Insurance Different?

Being an expert local agent and having experience in multi-line insurances makes a big difference. Instead of having to contact multiple brokers and agents for a single client, Kash Insurance offers comprehensive expertise that allows them to cover every aspect of their clients' insurance needs.

Clients prefer working with Kash Insurance because it is less time consuming, and people know they can be trusted due to their experience and knowledge.

A Personal Touch

The personal touch and personal consultant makes a huge difference when calling an 800 number. You go online and they know the difference of explaining all these options and coverage, the amount of coverage, and give you the ability to bundle your insurance with multiple insurances in one place and give the best deal as far as saving money, which at the end of the day is significant.

How To Find The Best Insurance

The best approach to choosing the correct insurance would be to consult and talk with a local expert so they could help you understand what you are looking for. They will ask questions, find out what your needs are, what type of insurance and coverage you need, how much to pay, and things like that in order to determine the best plan for you.

Dangers When Shopping For Insurance

There is a lot of false-advertising and insurance companies sometimes advertise something that is not available in that state.

You might call them up and ask for a quote, but then they might say that the policy you were calling about is not available in California, although it is in some other states. California is very big and it has a large population, so a lot of insurance companies have things that are provided in other states but they are not doing it in California.

When you see the quote, you also need to consider how the company would be able to pay the claim and whether it would be the replacement value or the cash value. People generally cannot understand these things by themselves, so it is always a good idea to show it to an expert in the industry who could explain whether you were not getting the best value for your dollar.

Insurance Made Easy

In addition to the 24-hour service offered by Farmers' Insurance, calls are directly routed to the claim service. All the evidence of insurance that is given to the client has the 24 hour phone number mentioned so they can contact their agent directly.

Clients can also go online and in many cases if they called during business hours, claims are taken immediately on the first call, where they will be opened, and then all the client has to do is wait for the adjuster to contact them and start the process.

Auto Insurance Services

For auto insurance clients, there are a number of body shops in different counties in Southern California that are Farmers' certified. People could just go directly to those offices and to those body shops and start repairing their cars and open their claim right there. The claims process offered is very smooth and has received positive feedback and many compliments from clients.

FIRST-TIME INSURANCE BUYERS

The bulk of business expansion and clientele comes to Kash Insurance through referrals, meaning most of their clients are looking for a better solution for their insurance, or they are seeking a better understanding of their insurance.

They are different from other companies because they spend time with their clients, reviewing their existing policies and trying to find a better solution as far as coverage, what is covered, what is not covered, how much coverage they need and how much would be at risk.

The client would be asked to answer a questionnaire so they could find the answer for them and provide them with the best package for their insurance needs.

Clients who do buy insurance for the first time might have moved from abroad, or they might have come from another state or another city. So they would need somebody who could help them understand local insurance policies and laws.

Importance Of Working With An Experienced Insurance Agent

You should definitely use someone experienced for your insurance needs because although you may have insurance, you might not know if you are covered in case of certain events.

People often buy insurance on the internet or through someone from an 800 number but they don't always have an understanding of what they should actually buy. They tend to just look at the price and think they are getting the best deal. In many instances they eliminate a lot of coverage from their insurance that they could have had at a slightly extra cost or maybe at no cost, so then even in case of a simple accident, they may find out they did not have enough coverage.

Finding The Right Coverage

In a lot of cases, they might have had a benefit that they did not know about, because nobody explained it to them. The important thing would be for you to find someone who could explain all of this to you and for the person you were asking to be an expert in this industry who could actually tell you and ask the right questions about your needs and situation.

Everybody's situation is different, which is why there is no one pick for everybody. Kash Insurance agents sit down with the client and ask them questions so they could find out how much deposit insurance they needed, which is why this would differ from person to person. What insurance is needed depends on the assets they were trying to protect because if they were at fault in an accident and if they did not have enough insurance, they would be liable to pay for those losses.

People and lawyers look for situations when one party is at fault so they can sue the person and come after their assets like their home equity, their business, and everything else. This is why it would be very important to have a considerable amount of and enough insurance to protect the person's assets, their family, and their future.

Most people do not understand their auto insurance coverage in regards to all the exclusions and all types of definitions as far as deductibles. They generally do not know how their insurance works.

A lot of the terms used are insurance terminologies and there are some technical and legal variables which can get confusing sometimes, which is why most people do not understand it. You would definitely need someone to help you understand all of this and you would need someone to lead you so that if you had a question, you could just pick up the phone and call them.

Misconceptions About Working With An Insurance Agent

One misconception is that people sometimes think they will have to pay a lot of money to someone to buy insurance, which would not be the case because an insurance agent would get paid by the insurance company, not the insured and not the consumer.

The other thing is that people think they need to shop around and then get the best deal out there, whereas by doing this, they would be missing a lot of other things such as a lot of benefits and coverage they could have gotten because they would have basically sacrificed those with the price.

Choosing Policy Over Price

It is a misconception that people think they can get the cheapest insurance with the best service, because that is just not possible, the reason being that there are a lot of requirements for a company to have the best service and to have the best claim service. For example, they would need to have enough staff to answer people when they call, and they would need a lot of other facilities that can help provide that kind of service to a client and those costs money.

An insurance company that wanted to provide this kind of service would have to keep their prices a little bit higher than competing companies who do not offer any services. There is always a reason for a price.

Kash Insurance is a service-based company, because there will always be a difference when you go to a high-end restaurant as compared to going to a Burger King. You would still be having food but in a high-end restaurant you would be paying for the service, the quality of the service, and the quality of the food. All insurance policies do not give the same coverage. They may have a common base, but there would be other exclusions and some other things that not every policy would cover.

In regards to price, you have to sacrifice a lot of things if you are just looking for the cheapest price.

AUTO POLICIES

The first thing that everybody talks about is auto insurance. It is mandatory to buy auto insurance in the state of California.

It is better to avoid the minimum type of policy because it offers very less insurance and a person would generally need a lot more than that to cover their assets if they got into an accident. The package policy for auto insurance offered by Kash covers liability, property, and uninsured motorist, along with other features such as rent-a-car, towing services, and so on.

The basic liability-only policy is for people who can only get liability if they had something like a very old car and they did not care if the car got totaled. If the car was not worth more than $2,000 to $3,000, they may want to consider just buying the liability only because the cost of the repair of that car, if it got in an accident, would perhaps be more than the whole price of the car, so we would be saving money by just buying the liability only policy.

Kash also offers auto insurance for high-end cars and luxury cars, along with auto insurance for classic cars in case someone was a collector. Besides that, they also have insurance packages for recreational vehicles.

Underinsured And Uninsured Motorist Coverage

You definitely need underinsured or uninsured driver coverage because it would not be applied automatically. The state of California does not employ it, but Kash does not sell any single policy without that.

Uninsured motorist and underinsured motorist coverage would basically be for when you were hit by another car whose driver did not have insurance or they did not have enough insurance. In that case, your insurance would cover you and the people in your car. It would pay for bodily injury and everything else in case there had been an accident.

Most people do not even know about uninsured or underinsured motorist coverage. Other people already have it, which is a good thing, but they do not know how useful it actually is. This is why it would always be better for people to work with an insurance agent, because the agent would be an expert in this and they would be able to help fill out the gaps.

Percentage Of People Who Are Uninsured Or Underinsured In California

This varies and changes from time to time because of factors like the economy and because of other factors involving the percentage of those who are uninsured or underinsured. The latest statistic shows that 15 to 20 percent of people have insurance and probably a larger percentage are underinsured as opposed to completely uninsured.

How Do Insurance Companies Assess A Persons' Risk As A Driver?

This would involve multiple factors and all insurance companies would legally need to judge this based on certain factors. California does not use any credit, although other states do. The zip code would be a factor because some areas see more accidents than others.

Secondly, the person's driving record would obviously need to be considered. By law in California, the person would not qualify for a good driver discount, which is usually 25 percent if they had a certain amount of tickets and/or accidents. They would also need to consider how old the person was and how many years of driving experience they have.

Minimum Liability In California

The minimum would be 15-30-5, which according to California Law, would require the minimum coverage to be $15,000 per person in an accident for liability only, $30,000 for total or bodily injury, and then $5,000 for damage to property, without requiring any uninsured motorist or anything like that.

You would not even need insurance if you put $36,000 in cash with the Department of Insurance in California, the DMV, so you could just provide evidence you deposited money in the DMV account.

This amount is actually an extreme minimum and it is too less because if you hit even the smallest car, you would have to pay $10,000 to $20,000 for the car. If you were at fault in the accident, then you would have to pay out of pocket if you did not have insurance.

Deductibles

Deductibles are one of the things that should always be discussed with the client. It is basically a self-retention amount, and it would also play a part in getting a better rate. Clients are always asked about their level of comfort and their ability to pay their deductible.

For example, someone could say they did not want to pay more than $250 out of pocket, or they might say it is just $100 or $500, whereas some people might say they simply do not care because in case of a major incident they would be okay with paying $1,000 or more.

People generally do not understand the amount of saving they could get and they could pay high deductibles but on the other hand, the affordability question would come in play too, which is why we do not have a standard deductible and it would just depend on the person's situation.

Does A Higher Deductible Automatically Mean Better Coverage?

No. The deductible would have nothing to do with the coverage, it would have to do with the price. The higher the deductible, the lower the premium. The person would pay less and end up with a high deductible and vice versa. Someone with a lower deductible would have to pay higher premiums.

Common Mistakes When Purchasing Insurance

A common mistake is when people are not too particular about the type of insurance, their self-retention amounts, or "Deductible." The deductible would be the amount of money they would have to pay out of pocket in case of an accident.

A lot of people want to keep the deductible as low as possible without considering the amount they could afford versus the money they were just paying more every month or every year.

A small deductible and that self-retention would help them not just save money on their premium, but also in the event there was a small claim, so they would not have to open a claim or pursue the claim because it would put a negative impact on their insurance for a few years.

Reasons Insurance Premiums Might Change

From time to time, insurance companies change their rates based on the amount of the claims they are bringing. They may have to increase their rates, not just for one person but for everybody, because of those claims so the cost of the insurance would go up for them.

Inflation would also affect this because of the cost of repairs. Your insurance would go up accordingly because the insurance company has to pay more even in a simple claim as compared to how much they would have to pay two years ago.

How To Get Discounts On Your Insurance Policy

You would basically be entitled to a continuous discount if you were a good driver and had no accidents.

The other thing would be to bundle the person's other insurance with one company. Most companies out there have a multi policy discount, meaning that if the person had more than one car, if they had a home or other assets to insure, then the company would give a multi-line insurance discount, which would be one of the things that could lower a person's cost of auto insurance.

Some companies, like Farmers' Insurance, give a discount to university graduates. If you have a Bachelor's degree or more, or if you are in a profession like lawyers, teachers, or doctors, then these would be extra discounts you could get.

Effects Of A DUI On Your Insurance Rate

People who get a DUI think that once they paid the fine, that would be it, whereas the DUI could stay on their record for up to 10 years and they would immediately lose their good driver discount. Some insurance companies would not even insure someone with a DUI.

You would definitely not be able to get insurance if you had two DUI's but in case you only had one, it would depend on the state and your record over the last 10 years. You would have to pay more premium every year just because that was on your record. Some people determine it would probably cost $200,000 overall in 10 years including all the fines, everything that would need to be paid, all the time you would lose off work plus the insurance and everything.

Can Traffic School Help Reduce Insurance Rates?

Yes, and you would be able to eliminate one ticket every 18 months. You would have to take a class, and pay the fine as well as for the class. If you have more than one ticket in 18 months, you would be able to get rid of one of them which would help because then your rate would not go up.

Clients who get a ticket are recommended to just go to class because otherwise, it would stay on their record for 3 years and they will end up paying more because they would have to pay the ticket anyway. You can do this class online nowadays and that will save you money.

Commercial Auto Insurance

There are passenger cars and commercial cars, and the type of insurance would depend on the size of the car and other criteria. Cars such as limousine, for example, are considered commercial vehicles, and you certainly could not buy personal auto insurance for some other vehicles like commercial trucks.

You would also have to buy commercial insurance if you were using your passenger car for a business, or if the car was registered under a business and it was being used as a business car. You would be in trouble if you did not do that because the insurance company would not cover any loss.

In case of personal auto insurance, the people who lived within the house would be added so they could also use the car, whereas with commercial insurance, you would basically have to add all your employees as drivers, provided they all drove cars. You would be able to get these flexibilities and you could also get higher coverage.

Does Commercial Insurance Cover Personal Use?

Yes. There would be no restriction if the person wanted to have their car covered for both business and personal use, because they could add personal use to the commercial coverage. Commercial automobile coverage would cover the same as the personal line of insurance would.

Would Commercial Cover?

Higher coverage means higher limits and it would also depend on the type of business you have. Obviously, for a taxi driver, their personal auto insurance would definitely not cover when they are driving people from one place to another, so this is something their commercial insurance would cover.

If you have a tow truck or a delivery truck, for example, then you would be getting more coverage because it would be commercial auto insurance. You may deliver business properties using your personal car, and those can be added to your commercial auto policy, which is something you cannot do in your personal line.

Motorcycle Insurance

Motorcycle insurance is similar to automobile insurance, but you would have to have a driver's license specifically for the motorcycle in order to get a discount.

Someone who wanted to buy motorcycle insurance would have around 60 days to get that license, although if they already had a license, and depending on how many years of experience they had, they may qualify for extra discounts as well. It would be the same in regards to coverage.

You would have to have the liability part, and you would be able to get a certain amount depending on how much the motorcycle was worth, and they could get the replacement cost or a cash value for it, which would be different than it is for cars. Some companies give just the replacement cost for most cars, whereas some companies give the cash value but there is basically more flexibility when it comes to motorcycles.

How Much Motorcycle Insurance Coverage Should Someone Have?

It would be the same as buying auto insurance in regards to liability limits, meaning how much you could damage someone's car if you were in an accident with them. The limit would usually be lower because in case of an accident, even if you hit a car, you as the motorcyclist would usually get more hurt than the person in the car or people in the car.

There is a minimum by the state law, and depending on the person's situation, they would be questioned about their assets and everything, so that they could be sure they were protected at minimum, or at least their assets were protected so that they would not be in trouble if they hit someone, so that insurance could pay in full for all the claims that came out of the accident.

There is sometimes collusion coverage and the questions of the deductible would also come into play. People sometimes forget they need to buy insurance for their motorcycle because it is not covered under their auto insurance.

HOME OWNER'S INSURANCE

By Law, Do I Need Home Owner's Insurance?

No, you would not legally need to have home owner's insurance.

People buy insurance for their homes for two major reasons. The first reason is because the bank would require them to get insurance when they obtained their loan to purchase a home. The second reason would be if the person wanted to protect their asset after their life of course and then co-owners.

The home owner would want to make sure that the home they were putting money in and that they have spent all their hard earning money to buy, will be there for them, their family or their next generation. It is an asset that can provide income and you would want to make sure it was protected against any unforeseen event and that there would be a claim if there was any damage.

Coverage Under A Home Insurance Policy

Some people say one of the more important aspects in your lifetime is your home, so you want to make sure you are covering that against losses, against claims, and against catastrophic events. The basic home owner's policy will cover you against fire, water damage, vandalism, wind, hail, and theft.

Some policies do not cover theft. Some policies do not cover water damage and they might have limited coverage on some other things like vandalism, although generally speaking, the basic coverage for a home owner's insurance would be fire insurance because sometimes "Fire Insurance" is said in place of home owner's insurance.

A simple home owner's insurance would be fire insurance because that is the main thing that would need to be covered and most lenders or some banks who may need to give you a loan would care about fire insurance.

Things Not Covered Under Home Owners Insurance

The most important thing is first of all, if you are living in that house, you should make sure you have a full package insurance which covers also theft, water damage and everything else. You should make sure it includes personal properties, like all your belongings, some exclusion on jewelries, fine arts, watches, firearms and all of that.

Limited coverage between $1,500 to $5,000 would be included in most policies. If you had more than that or if things like jewelry, fine art or antiques were worth more than $5,000, then you would definitely need to get a floater for your policy or you could add a specific coverage limit and amount to the policy and then get enough coverage to cover those in case of a loss.

These items can be discussed either in person or over the phone to be sure they are sufficiently covered in your insurance policy.

Do I Need To Take Inventory And Photographs Of Belongings?

Yes, because you want to make sure you get exactly what you lost, and that you were getting a full amount which is why you should make sure you have an inventory list. That is what you will bear and in case of a total loss or any loss, it would basically cover everything you have up to the personal value.

Choosing The Right Home Owner's Insurance

You should look for an A+ rated company that you know has been in business for a long time so that in the case of a loss, you will still get paid. You should not just buy insurance, you should make sure you are insured and you should review your coverage with an expert.

What Is Included In A Home Owner's Insurance Policy?

There are different parts. The first part is coverage A, which covers the building and then there would be the Coverage B, which refers to a separate structure. Some people have a warehouse or a garage that is not attached to the building, so those second parts of the policy would always be included in your policy. You would not have to buy secondary insurance for that additional structure.

The third part would be the personal property or the contents in the home, like clothes, furniture, and everything else you own. Anything you can move with you would be considered personal property.

The other part would be the loss of use in case there is a fire or water damage so you were not able to live in the house for a certain amount of time. The policy would pay for your expenses to go in a hotel or rent another apartment for a while till you could rebuild or restore your house.

Earthquake Coverage

Earthquake insurance, by itself, is a standalone policy that can be added to your package, but it would not be a part of your home owner's policy. It would cover earthquakes and there would normally be a high deductible for earthquake insurance.

Requests for earthquake insurance have become more frequent. Anytime an earthquake takes place, ten calls or more are placed the next day requesting coverage for this disaster. The rate has been decreased and some insurance companies, like Farmers Insurance, offer a discount on home owners' insurance, which is something that has just happened this year.

Common Property Insurance Claims

The most common property insurance claims are water damage and fire, depending on where you are in California.

Water damage is the most common and it would depend on how bad it is and how long it had been going on. If a pipe broke while you were on vacation, then your house would be underwater by the time you came back. It would be covered and probably restored in a short time if it was just an additional pipe, but even a larger claim would usually be resolved within one week or two depending on how big the claim was. Farmers Insurance claims department team is on call 24-hours, and they can come to you and take care of everything.

Deductibles For Home Owners

Recently, some insurance companies have come up with different types of deductibles. It used to be a fixed dollar amount which would start from $100 and it would go up to $5,000 or $10,000, but nowadays, it is calculated based on a percentage which starts from half a percent and goes to 10 percent in some areas, although that is rare. People usually feel comfortable with a fixed dollar amount of $1,000, $2,000, $3,000 or $5,000.

Liability Under Home Owner's Insurance

Liability is basically something that comes with all home owner policies. It could be optional, but it is rarely included in any policy that clients would not want.

You would want to buy a liability with your home owners policy because that would be a kind of personal liability as well, meaning if there was a fire from your house that went to the next house and the next house, then the liability part of the policy would pay for those assets. It would also cover damages if someone came to your property and got hurt.

Protection Against Liability Claims

On the liability side, besides the home owners insurance you would have a liability, which would usually start from $100,000 worth of coverage and it would go to a million, but what would happen if you needed more liability and in case the claim could not be covered by home owner's insurance because of the nature of the claim.

Some exclusions would not be covered by a simple home owner's policy or auto insurance. With regards to the liability, we would firstly have to consider the exclusion and secondly, we would have to see the amount of the loss.

In some cases involving a lawsuit, your $100,000 or $300,000 or $500,000 worth of liability insurance would not pay or it would not be enough to pay the whole claim. In that scenario, you could get another type of insurance called Umbrella Insurance.

Umbrella Coverage

The Umbrella Policy is actually a separate policy that goes above and beyond your underlying auto and home owner's policy. It will typically cover all your vehicles, all your homes, motorcycle, vacant lands, and anything you have, which is why it is called an Umbrella because it covers everything.

The minimum coverage is usually $1 million but it can go up to $5, $10 and $15 million. It not only goes over the limit of the policy, but also covers more as far as the dollar amount and it also covers all the exclusions you might have on your home owners and auto insurance and so forth. In many cases, we recommend an umbrella policy to cover everything else.

How Do Prior Home Loss Or Claims Impact Someone's Rate?

In California especially, some insurance companies will avoid insuring your house if you have more than the one or two losses, because this would impact your rate and impact you overall. It would raise the rate for up to 3 years.

What Would The Home Owner's Premium Depend On?

The first thing that the premium would depend on would be the amount of coverage, how much coverage you were buying and the size of the house because the coverage A, which is the dwelling and it covers the building, would be the amount of insurance you were purchasing for your house in case of total loss.

In California, a single family house would usually cost $400,000 to 500,000 on average and up to $7 to $8,00,000. This is the main thing that affects the premium, as well as the location of the property.

High-Risk Areas

If you are in a fire zone place, meaning if there was the possibility of a fire, or if the house was far from the nearest fire station, then those factors would need to be considered and you may end up paying more premium in those scenarios versus in the low risk area, where you would obviously pay less.

Deductibles And Discounts

The deductible would be a factor as well. In many cases, a certain deductible would give the best price but this would vary from company to company and this is usually something we would explain to our client. Home owner's insurance, auto insurance, and life insurance would give you more of a discount, which is why it is very important to check about all these possibilities so you can get not only the best coverage and the best policy but also have the best price.

BUSINESS INSURANCE

Business insurance itself is not mandatory, although many businesses buy business insurance for liability and property. When starting a business, you would want to protect yourself against lawsuits and any type of liability arising out of the business operation.

Types of Business Insurance

There are a variety of business insurances but in any case, the business liability policy, business owner's policy and the business property, could be included in one policy, although some companies do it separately.

It is important to first find out what kind of business insurance someone needs after sitting down with the business owners and asking them questions and all of that, so the agent could make sure they provide them the business insurance they need to make sure their business is protected. This puts them at ease so they can just focus on their business and make money.

Is Insurance A Legal Requirement For Businesses?

Not legally. There are obviously many sorts of business insurance but as far as legality, the only insurance they would need to have is worker's compensation insurance if they have employees. Other types of insurances are not legally required, when leasing a space or buying a business that required a 10-year loan against it.

Choosing The Right Insurance For Your Business

Different types of insurance would be needed depending on whether it was a startup business or an existing business and if it was in one location or multiple locations, because that would need different types of insurance and coverage. It would also depend on if they owned the building, or if they had a lot of equipment, the contents they have, what is addressed, and what kind of operation they have.

There are a lot of varieties of business insurance and a lot of things can be changed and varied. You should have an insurance expert explain all of these because they could provide you with different packages, which is what is offered at Kash Insurance Agency.

We provide a lot of different packages to our clients to make sure they are covered in regards to everything that could harm the business.

What Is Workers' Comp?

All employers in California are required to buy workers' comp insurance to basically cover all medical costs and indemnity for the injured worker. It would cover the work duration, meaning any injuries that came out from the work no matter who was at fault. If a worker got injured, the insurance policy would pay for all the medical and indemnity costs to the employee. It can get expensive, depending on the type of industry, the employer's experience, and how many claims the company had and issues like that, so it can get a little bit complicated. It is mandatory and it is getting more expensive, especially these days.

Affordability Of Workers' Compensation

The employer would have to pay a percentage of the salary for workers' compensation insurance, so the cost would depend on how many employees they have and the payroll amount.

It has been going on forever and in some cases it can really get expensive so the employer may not be able to afford it, which is why some businesses reduce their employee size by firing people. It is important to have an insurance expert help businesses keep that cost as low as possible or else it would affect their overall operation.

Factors To Consider When Buying Business Insurance

The lender or landlord would have certain requirements for basic things like liability and some property coverage that would have to be met if someone was getting a loan or leasing a space.

The business would also need coverage against other things like theft, vandalism, employee dishonesty and other things. Some policies would just cover a basic general liability in case the business had a claim because of their product or course of operation.

People do not know about these things and they would need an expert in that industry to ask some questions from and who could tell them about the claims they have seen, and to find out of the person was aware of certain things and if they knew they could get sued.

At Kash Insurance, agents can add and delete things from the package but the client would always need to see it through an expert's eye.

Keyman's Insurance

A lot of business owners do not think about appointing someone incase something happened to them or if something happened to their manager or someone who was running their business. They do not think about who would be next to take charge and how much they might lose or that they may even go out of business if that key person was not in place.

Keyman life insurance is purchased by the business for the manager or the owner, or it could also be for partners so they would be protected. If that person passed away, the insurance policy would pay the beneficiary, meaning the business, so it could use that money to stay in business, operate and find another person to replace the person for whom insurance had been bought earlier.

Comprehensive Coverage For All Business Risks

We would put together a package to cover everything after asking questions and finding out the needs of the business. There is no standard comprehensive insurance policy for each business, although it could be made comprehensive for each situation. You would have to get a comprehensive package and you would have to have an expert help you put it together.

How Much Liability Insurance Do I Really Need?

This would depend on the size of the business and size of their assets. The general liability starts with $500,000 per accident and it would go up to $2 million in most cases.

We have half a million, $1 million, and then $2 million, and most of the requirement from the banks and from the landlords is really a minimum of $1 million. Nobody really gets this lower than $1 million because there would be no difference if you wanted to get lower than $1 million. There is usually no difference or just a very tiny difference in the premium, which is why you would then decide to just get the $1 million, which is a common minimum for business insurance as far as liability.

Other Factors

The rest of the policy coverage would just depend on if you owned the building, if the lease required you to have the insurance for the building, and also how much content you had and how much risk you wanted to take for yourself. Some people are risk takers, which is not recommended at all.

These kinds of people say they would not care if anything happened, but when something did happen, they would realize what a big mistake they had made by not having the insurance or not having enough insurance because they would end up having to pay out of their pocket to cover all the losses.

Professional Liability Insurance

Professional liability insurance is different than other kinds of insurance. It is basically for certain types of businesses, for example, lawyers, doctors, realtors and insurance agents. There is a kind of professional liability known as "errors and omissions" or for doctors, it is called "Malpractice Insurance," and this would all go under professional liability insurance.

If it was a standalone policy for itself and had different types of limits and deductibles and all of that and by itself also had other criteria and other exclusions that defined the other things it covered, then it would basically cover all the operations concerning certain types of business regarding covering mistakes and errors of the insured.

If something happened that was the fault of the insured, the insurance company would pay that claim to the consumer or to the person who got hurt.

Umbrella Insurance Policies For Businesses

There are umbrella insurance policies for businesses. Business policies are more comprehensive than an auto or home owner policy. A lot of things are already covered under those policies but the limitations on a business policy would usually only allow you to buy up to $2 million on liability.

If you needed more liability because of multiple assets or there were a lot of things at risk, then you would need to buy an umbrella policy because that would go above and beyond the current liability policy and it would give more coverage in case of a lawsuit or loss.

Customized Policies And Insurance Packages

Custom policy packages can be developed based on your needs in case you are a startup business, an online business, or in some cases, if the business was facing a multi-state risk, due to completing businesses in different states.

MEDICARE

Medicare comes from the government, and you would have to be 65 years old in order to qualify for it. Part A and part B are provided by the government, so you would not have to pay for it, whereas you could purchase part C and D through private insurance companies. This would cover doctor visits, medication, and so forth.

To qualify for Medicare in the first place, you would have to have at least 10 years of work and of paying taxes and you would also have to be of certain age. Early disability would also be a qualifying event.

Why Purchase Additional Medicare?

You do not have to, but since Medicare would cover 80 percent of the costs, you would have to pay the remaining 20 percent of the costs out of pocket. You should buy another private insurance to cover that 20 percent.

There is a medical supplemental insurance which covers that 20 percent, and there is medical advantage which covers not only that part of supplemental but it also covers the drug benefit, which is something you need to have, because without it you would have to pay for the 20 percent for the prescription drugs and for doctor's visits.

How Complex Is Health Care?

Medical insurance or health insurance is a very important insurance to have.

It is complicated sometimes, so insurance companies are required to make it simpler so everybody can understand, which is why a lot of people choose to get consultant for getting this type of insurance.

Obama Care

Everything has changed primarily to the benefit of the consumers and individuals with these ACA changes, also known as Obama Care. In the past, when you wanted to buy insurance, there were exclusions regarding what the health insurance would cover and which hospital the person could go to.

With the changes of the ACA, or Affordability Care Act, everything has changed and there is a standard coverage on all policies. All policies have to cover hospitalization, doctor visits, delivery of a baby, and all of that whether you need it or not.

You might want some extra coverage like visiting an acupuncturist or a chiropractor or something like that. Not every policy has this, but you could certainly get an insurance policy and get those coverage as well.

Is Health Insurance Affordable?

It would then become a question of the premiums and how much you would have to pay every month. The changes of the industry and the government are trying to make it affordable for everybody to purchase insurance. If you cannot pay the full premium or if your income does not let you to pay the full premium, then you can get a subsidy from the government which would make it affordable to purchase insurance.

It has been advertised heavily in the past years, so a lot of people know there is help out there.

Can I Get Insurance Through My Employer?

Of course you could get it through your employer and you could participate if they were providing you with the group health insurance. Those would usually be more comprehensive insurances as far as coverage. Clients are always advised to just go with an employer sponsored plan and get it through their employer.

In some cases, they decide they want to get their own policy and their own insurance, which is there the topic of affordability and which insurance to choose comes up.

How To Get Health Insurance That Fits Your Budget

Medicare and those other related Medicare insurances would apply after the age of 65, so before that, you should always have medical insurance which could get more expensive and especially now, it is required by law for everybody to have medical insurance; otherwise they will be penalized and at the end of the year, they would have

to pay a penalty for not having the medical insurance.

The affordability law has passed also, so basically depending on how much you made in a year, you would not have to pay more than 9.9 percent of your income for health insurance.

If someone made $36,000 a year, then the maximum they would have to pay for the insurance would be under 9.9 percent. This would wholly be calculated by net income, so if the net income was $36,000 then they would have to pay $3,600 for the whole year. If they got a plan for $500 a month, they would just pay the $300 and then the rest would be paid through the government.

In some cases people are paying $50 or $20 a month to get the health insurance, whereas it was not possible to get that price for medical insurance 2 or 3 years ago.

Medicaid and Medical

If your income is under a certain amount, then depending on the state, you would get free medical insurance, or Medicaid. In California, we call it Medical, whereas it is Medicaid in other states, and it is basically You would be able to get Medical or Medicaid if your income did not qualify you to purchase insurance.

At this point, everybody can get it, although there could be situations where multiple members of the family did not qualify for Medical or Medicaid but they still had to pay but then their income did not let them pay. This is now rare, thanks to the government's help, but it is something that is under discussion.

Life Insurance

This is a must have insurance for everybody, because the most important asset in anyone's life is themselves. If you would buy insurance for your car, your home, your boat or your motorcycle, then you should definitely buy insurance for yourself.

This is especially important if you have a family, when you have people to care for or if you are the sole provider to a family. You should make some provision in case you do not come back home the next day so everything like your child's care, the food, the mortgage, the rent, or everything else would be paid for.

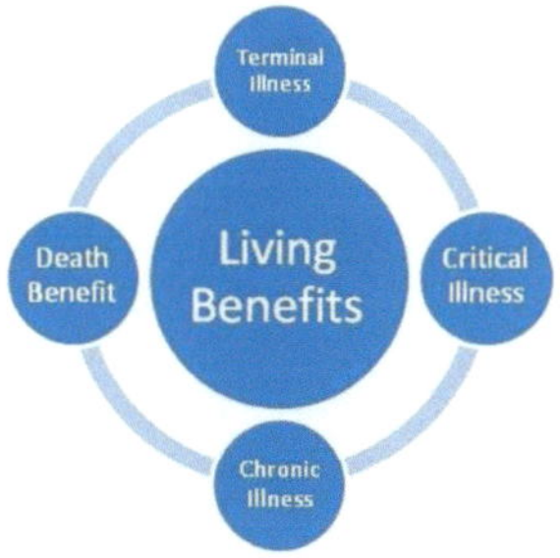

Benefits of Life Insurance

A life insurance policy would pay the beneficiaries the amount of the coverage and you could secure a big chunk of money by paying pennies on the dollar every month. Pennies on the dollar really means pennies on the dollar. The amount of coverage you can secure for your family can be paid to your beneficiaries if you die and it could be huge and it would make a huge difference if you do not have life insurance.

Families have been devastated because they lost their dad or mom and they did not know what to do. The money is not taxable, meaning it is actually tax free money to your family and nothing would be deducted from that amount.

Some people think everything will be fine because they have savings. The question is how much money they can put in the bank and how much would they be able to make on that money because at the end, they would still have to pay taxes on that.

A life insurance policy could help a lot if something happened to the family.

When To Get Life Insurance

People tend to think about it when they get old, which is a big mistake because it would be more expensive for someone who was older. It would also be more difficult to qualify for life insurance if there is something wrong with your body like an illness or a disease. Insurance should be started when you are young and healthy, like when you are in your 30s or 40s.

There are obviously different types of life insurances, but as far as the age goes, the best time to get life insurance would be as early as possible and the best time would be when you are young and healthy.

Types Of Life Insurance Policies

We generally have two types of life insurances, one is a term insurance and the other is a permanent Life Insurance.

Renewable Term Life Insurance

Most insurance policies and term life insurances are renewable. There is no cash value in the term insurance policy, so you would just pay your premium every month and then the policy would expire at certain time. You could extend it or renew it and you would have to pay a higher premium at that time.

There is a conversion feature in most term insurance policies so that you could convert that policy to a permanent policy before the policy expired and before a certain age, you would be able to do that without taking any medical test or any re-qualification, which is a big benefit because you do not know what happens in your life. If something happened like you got sick, then you would have a lot of trouble to get qualified again for life

insurance, and so the best thing to do would be to just convert it.

The term insurance is for a certain amount of time. It would usually start from 5 years and could be for up to 30 years. You would buy insurance for that period of time and the policy would expire after that time, and you would pay a fixed dollar amount every month for all these years to keep that policy enforced. It would be better to buy insurance for a certain amount of time that you feel comfortable with and that you know you'll need it for.

Why Buy Term Insurance?

People buy term insurance for many reasons which would depend on their situation. It would also depend on how much they could afford. It would depend on how old you are and what is the goal, what you are trying to protect and for how long you are trying to protect it, how old your children are, and what is the purpose of buying the life insurance.

In case you wanted to buy a term Life Insurance, you would have to ask certain questions in order to determine how much life insurance you needed, and for how long.

Permanent Insurance

Permanent life insurance is a policy that will last your whole life, meaning it would not expire. It would pay out when you die. People are always recommended to buy permanent life insurance because it is what they need and it is what they will use.

You could buy auto insurance, home owner's insurance, or business insurance, but unless something happened, you would never actually use it. It would just protect you until you had a claim, so you would have that peace of mind. Permanent life insurance is the only insurance you would definitely use because death is something that happens to everybody.

Besides the term being permanent, a proportion of the money you pay every month as your premium to the insurance company would be invested in some other assets, liquid assets like cash or mutual funds and bonds. The insurance company would basically pay you a dividend or interest on your money depending on how much they made.

Some insurance companies or some insurance policies have a certain guaranteed percentage, like 4 to 8 percent. They may pay more but they have a base rate guaranteed on the money that you would be investing in your life insurance policy.

Why Choose A Permanent Life Insurance Policy?

There is a cost of insurance as well. A portion of your money would go toward the cost of insurance like the term insurance and then the rest of it would go for investment. Permanent life insurance has a lot of good features that regular term insurance does not have.

You could get a loan against your policy, you could take the money and use it for any other purpose you wanted and after a certain number of years, there would be no tax consequences as well, so the money you took out from your life insurance after a certain number of years would not be taxable at all.

Even if you did not touch that money, certain policies could add those cash values with the money you pay every month, and it would go to a Cash Value Account. The cash value account would keep increasing so the death benefit would be increased.

The permanent life policy has a lot of good features and benefits that you cannot get through the term and policy.

Cancelling And Expired Policies

You could cancel the policy anytime because it is a month to month policy. All life insurances are month to month as far as the obligation to pay the premium. Statistics show that on average, people buy life insurance 7 times in their lives in America because they cancel it or it lapses or whatever reason, so they then buy another one, or they may buy multiple policies and keep some of them or cancel or they keep all of them.

A large percentage of term insurance policies lapse for multiple reasons. People buy the term insurance and they might not need it anymore so they just cancel it, or they just do not pay it and it gets lapsed because in term insurance, there is no value as far as cash in it, so if you do not pay, you do not have it. It is just like auto insurance or home owners insurance.

With permanent insurance, the percentage of lapse is a lot less than term insurance because there is value into it and people do not want to lose the money they have there. Of course they would be able to cash it out, and they could take the money because whatever money was there would be their money. They could cash it out and cancel it, but they keep it because they seek the value in the permanent insurance and it would stay with them until they need it.

Factors To Consider Before Buying Insurance

You should firstly consider the amount of insurance you want to buy. You should make sure you are buying enough because the statistics say that more than 50 to 70 percent who have life insurance do not have enough life insurance.

You should also consider the type of the policy, how long you will need this policy, and what the purpose of it would be, whether it would be protecting your family or protecting your assets, or if there was a tax benefit to it as well.

This would all need to be considered, and when talking about life insurance, retirement would also come in place, so that would also need to go into the estate planning. Life insurance plays a big role in estate planning as well.

Mistakes Made When Purchasing Life Insurance

People sometimes just go after the price, which is a common mistake because they do not see the company's financial history and how long the company had been in business because that would be important.

The most important insurance in your life is your life insurance. If the company went out of the business or something happened to the company and then you died, they would not pay. A financially savvy company would be able to pay all their obligations, which is why that should be the first thing you should see when buying life insurance.

This would matter especially when it come to a permanent policy, because you would be able to add some features in the added benefit to your policy, for example, long term care or disability or income riders, or a certain or critical illness.

Some of these are free so you would only need to apply for them. In some cases, you would have to pay just a little bit more to have those benefits in your policy, which is why you should not buy it over the phone or over the internet and it would be better to consult with an expert before buying.

Made in the USA
Las Vegas, NV
10 November 2026

57858447R00036